AI: The New Revolution

A complete guide to understand and use Artificial Intelligence

By

Julien MATTEI

Disclaimer:
The information provided in this book is intended for educational and informational purposes only. While the author and publisher have made every effort to ensure the accuracy and completeness of the information contained within, they make no guarantee or warranty, express or implied, concerning the applicability, suitability, or accuracy of the information for any specific purpose. The author and publisher shall not be held responsible or liable for any errors, omissions, or inaccuracies in the content, nor for any actions taken in reliance thereon.

This book does not provide professional, legal, or financial advice. The reader is advised to consult with a qualified professional before making any decisions or taking any actions based on the information provided herein. The author and publisher shall not be held liable for any loss, damage, or injury, direct or indirect, arising out of the use or misuse of the information contained in this book.

Summary

Introduction

Congratulations on taking the first step towards unlocking the true potential of Artificial Intelligence by investing in this comprehensive guide! As a reader, you have demonstrated your curiosity and commitment to understanding the world of AI and its immense possibilities. This book is designed to be your trusted companion on this exciting journey, offering a deep dive into the core concepts, applications, and ethical implications of AI technology.

Artificial Intelligence has rapidly evolved from a niche subject to a transformative force that shapes our everyday lives. In this ever-changing landscape, it is crucial to stay informed and develop a strong foundation in AI principles. This book will provide you with the knowledge and insights required to navigate the AI ecosystem with confidence and capitalize on the opportunities it presents.

In the pages that follow, we will explore the history of AI, its underlying technologies, and the wide array of real-world applications across various industries. We will also share best practices for leveraging AI in your projects and discuss the ethical considerations that must be taken into account when developing and deploying AI solutions.

So, let us embark on this fascinating journey together! As you immerse yourself in the world of Artificial Intelligence, you will not only gain valuable knowledge but also empower yourself to harness the transformative power of AI in your personal and professional endeavors. Turn the page, and let's begin our exploration of the future of technology.

CHAPTER ONE

INTRODUCTION TO AI

Chapter one: Introduction to AI

1.1: History and Development of AI Language Models

Let's start by answering what it is and where it come from.

A brief look in a dictionary will give you this definition:

Artificial Intelligence - The capacity of computers or other machines to exhibit or simulate intelligent behavior; the field of study concerned with this. Abbreviated *AI*.

Now that we have a basic understanding of the term, we will have a quick history lesson to better understand what it is.

The concept of artificial intelligence (AI) can be traced back to ancient times, with early myths and stories featuring automatons and other artificial beings. However, it wasn't until the mid-20th century that the field of AI as we know it today began to take shape.

We can divide in 5 periods the technical evolutions of AI research:

The first period covers the early ideas and concepts from ancient times to mid 20th century. The idea of creating machines that could mimic human intelligence has been around for centuries. Ancient myths and stories often featured automatons and other artificial beings that could think and act independently. These early ideas and concepts paved the way for the development of AI as we know it today.

The second period is about the birth of AI research. The 1950s marked the beginning of formal AI research, with the Dartmouth Conference in 1956 being a pivotal moment. The term "artificial intelligence" was coined during this conference, and it brought together leading minds in computing to discuss the potential of intelligent machines. Early AI research focused on creating machines that could learn, problem-solve, and understand natural language.

Following this, it was the period of AI's early successes and setbacks from the 60's to the 80's. During this period, AI research began to show promising results, with early successes in areas such as natural language processing, expert systems, and robotics. However, the field also faced challenges, including a lack of funding and the limitations of available computing power. These setbacks led to a temporary slowdown in AI research, known as the "AI winter."

As after any winter came spring and with it the rise of machine learning from the end of the 80's to the 2000's. The development of machine learning techniques, particularly neural networks, reinvigorated AI research in the late 1980s. This stage saw significant advancements in AI's ability to recognize patterns, learn from data, and improve over time. In early 90's, appeared Deep Blue, an AI famous for beating chess grandmaster Kasparov. The increasing availability of powerful computers and large datasets allowed researchers to develop more sophisticated machine learning algorithms, fueling further progress in the field.

Finally, our era, a time where terms like deep learning and AGI (Artificial General Intelligence) came at the forefront. The 2010s marked the beginning of the deep learning revolution, which has been responsible for many of the most significant AI breakthroughs in recent years. Deep learning techniques, which involve training large neural networks to recognize complex patterns, have led to remarkable advancements in areas such as image and speech recognition, natural language processing, and autonomous systems. Most recent model like GPT4 have been labelled by researchers as the first early but still uncomplete example of an Artificial General Intelligence, an AI that can apply intelligence to a large variety of problems, in similar fashion a human would do. Today, AI continues to evolve rapidly, with researchers exploring new techniques and applications that promise to transform our world in the years to come.

1.2: Architecture and Functioning of GPT-like Models:

GPT-like models are at the forefront of AI language research, offering impressive language understanding and generation capabilities. In this chapter, we'll break down the architecture and functioning of these models in a way that's easy for anyone to understand.

The Building Blocks: Neurons and Layers

Imagine that GPT-like models are like a giant stack of pancakes. Each pancake represents a layer, and within each layer, there are many tiny dots called neurons. These neurons are inspired by the cells in our brains and are responsible for processing information.

The bottom pancakes in the stack represent the initial layers of the model. These layers are responsible for learning the basic elements of language, such as grammar, syntax, and common word associations. By working together, these foundational layers allow the model to grasp the fundamental structure of the language.

As we move up the stack, the middle pancakes, or layers, start learning more complex language patterns and relationships. They begin to understand the context, semantics, and intricacies of the language. These layers also help the model grasp more abstract concepts, like sarcasm, humor, and cultural references.

The top pancakes in the stack represent the final layers of the model. These layers are responsible for refining the model's understanding and generation of language. They help to fine-tune the model's output, ensuring it is coherent, relevant, and engaging. The top layers are also crucial for adapting the model to specific tasks, such as translation or summarization, through the fine-tuning process.

To complete our pancake metaphor, imagine the syrup poured over the stack as the connections between the neurons within the layers. The syrup spreads across each pancake, connecting all the layers and allowing them to work together seamlessly. These connections help the model to process, learn, and generate language more effectively.

Learning from Data: Training the Model

To make GPT-like models understand and generate human-like language, we need to teach them using lots of data. This process is called training. During training, the model reads countless sentences and phrases from books, articles, and websites. It then adjusts the connections between the neurons to learn the patterns and structures in the text.

Decoding Language: Tokenization

GPT-like models don't understand words the same way we do. Instead, they break words and sentences into smaller pieces called tokens. Tokens can be as short as one letter or as long as a whole word. By using tokens, the model can understand the relationships between different words and phrases in a more efficient way.

The Magic of Prediction: Generating Text

Once the model is trained, it can generate new text by predicting the next token in a sequence. For example, if you give the model the phrase "The cat is", it will use its knowledge to guess the next token, such as "sleeping" or "hungry." The model can continue predicting tokens to generate complete sentences, paragraphs, or even longer text.

Adapting to Different Tasks: Fine-Tuning

GPT-like models can be adapted to various tasks, such as translation, summarization, or answering questions. To achieve this, the model undergoes a process called fine-tuning. Fine-tuning is like giving the model additional training with specific examples of the task you want it to perform. This helps the model to become more specialized and accurate in that particular task.

In conclusion, GPT-like models are an exciting and powerful tool in the world of AI language processing. They consist of multiple layers filled with neurons that work together to understand and generate human-like language. By training and fine-tuning these models with massive amounts of data, we've been able to create AI systems that can perform a wide variety of language tasks with remarkable accuracy.

1.3: Limitations and Future Directions

Artificial intelligence (AI) has made remarkable progress in recent years, transforming industries and reshaping the way we interact with technology. Despite these achievements, AI is far from perfect and still faces significant challenges. In this part, we will explore some of the key limitations of AI, delve into the concept of Artificial General Intelligence (AGI), and examine the possible future directions of AI development.

One of the main limitations of AI is its narrow focus. Current AI systems are highly specialized, designed to excel in specific tasks or domains. For example, a model that can recognize objects in images may not be able to understand natural language or play chess. This limited scope means that AI systems have constraints on their adaptability and versatility, which can hinder their practical applications in diverse situations.

Another issue with AI models is their lack of true understanding. These models can identify patterns and make predictions, but they do not possess the ability to understand the underlying meaning or context of the data they process. Consequently, AI systems may draw incorrect conclusions or make errors when faced with unfamiliar or ambiguous inputs.

Bias and fairness also present challenges for AI. Systems can inadvertently learn and perpetuate biases found in their training data, resulting in unfair or discriminatory outcomes. Addressing bias and ensuring fairness in AI systems is an ongoing area of research and development that holds ethical significance.

Furthermore, AI models typically require large amounts of data to learn and perform well. Acquiring and curating high-quality data can be both time-consuming and expensive. Privacy concerns and data protection regulations may also restrict access to certain types of data, which can hinder AI model development and deployment. Finally, the explainability and interpretability of AI models can be problematic. The inner workings of AI models, especially deep learning models, can be complex and difficult to understand. This lack of transparency, often referred to as the "black box" problem, makes it challenging to trust AI systems, diagnose errors, and ensure accountability.

While current AI systems excel in specific tasks, they lack the broad cognitive capabilities of humans. The concept of Artificial General Intelligence (AGI) envisions an AI system possessing general intelligence comparable to human intelligence, enabling it to learn, reason, and adapt across a wide range of tasks and domains. Achieving AGI is considered the ultimate goal of AI research. Developing AGI would require breakthroughs in our understanding of intelligence, learning, and cognition, as well as advances in AI algorithms, hardware, and data resources.

Looking forward, research efforts will likely continue to push towards the development of AGI. This may involve integrating multiple specialized AI systems, creating more adaptive and versatile learning algorithms, and incorporating insights from neuroscience, cognitive science, and psychology. In addition, researchers will work on addressing the limitations of current AI systems, developing techniques to reduce data dependency, improve explainability and interpretability, and tackle bias and fairness concerns.

As AI systems become more capable, they will increasingly collaborate with humans to enhance human decision-making and problem-solving. This will involve developing AI systems that can understand and adapt to human preferences, values, and emotions, as well as advances in human-computer interaction.

Moreover, as AI becomes more pervasive, there will be growing attention to the ethical implications of AI systems and the need for regulation to ensure responsible use. This may include the development of AI ethics guidelines, standards, and legal frameworks, as well as efforts to promote transparency, accountability, and public understanding of AI technologies.

Finally, AI will continue to play a significant role in emerging technologies, driving innovation in fields such as healthcare, transportation, and environmental management. As AI technology advances, so will its potential to address some of the most pressing challenges facing mankind.

CHAPTER TWO

THE IMPORTANCE OF EFFECTIVE COMMUNICATION

Chapter two: The Importance of Effective Communication

2.1: The Role of Communication in Achieving Desired Outcomes

Effective communication is essential for achieving desired outcomes, not only in human interactions but also when engaging with artificial intelligence (AI) systems like ChatGPT. In this chapter we will explore the fundamental principles of communication with AI, examine its impact on obtaining desired results, and discuss strategies for improving communication effectiveness with ChatGPT.

At its core, communication with AI involves the exchange of information, requests, and instructions between a user and an AI system. The user, acting as the sender, formulates a query or command, which the AI system, acting as the receiver, decodes and interprets. Successful communication depends on the accurate transmission and comprehension of these messages, which can be influenced by factors such as clarity, context, and the AI's underlying knowledge and capabilities.

One of the most critical aspects of communication in achieving desired outcomes with AI systems like ChatGPT is the establishment of shared understanding. When users can effectively convey their questions, intentions, and expectations, they create a basis for mutual understanding and cooperation. This shared understanding allows the AI system to align its responses with the user's goals, providing more accurate and relevant information or assistance.

In interactions with ChatGPT, effective communication fosters a productive and satisfying user experience. By clearly expressing their needs and objectives, users enable ChatGPT to better understand the context and deliver appropriate responses. This understanding helps avoid misinterpretations and ensures that the AI system can provide valuable input, suggestions, or solutions.

Users should aim to make their queries or commands as clear and specific as possible. This includes providing enough context for the AI system to understand the request and using precise language to describe the desired outcome.

If a user's initial query does not yield the desired response, they can provide additional information or context in a follow-up message. This iterative approach can help refine the AI system's understanding of the user's needs and improve its ability to provide relevant responses.

Users can experiment with different phrasings, keywords, or question formats to find the most effective way to communicate their requests. Sometimes, slight changes in wording can yield significantly better results.

Providing feedback on AI system responses can help improve the model's understanding of user expectations and adapt its future responses accordingly. Constructive feedback enables AI developers to refine and enhance the AI system's capabilities, ultimately leading to better communication and desired outcomes. It can be done directly by telling the AI what I could have done better or sometimes also via a upvote or downvote system build in the AI.

You will find detailed phrasing and examples later in this book for the use of ChatGPT and other AI solutions.

2.2: Miscommunication Examples and Potential Consequences

Despite recent progress, AI systems are still prone to miscommunication, which can lead to unintended consequences. We will explore several examples of miscommunication with AI systems and the potential consequences that can arise from these misunderstandings.

One common source of miscommunication with AI systems is the use of ambiguous language or the lack of context in user queries or commands. Ambiguity can cause AI systems like ChatGPT to misinterpret the user's intent or provide irrelevant or inappropriate responses.

Example: A user asks an AI system, "What's the best way to the city?" The AI system may interpret this request in various ways, such as providing directions to a specific city or offering suggestions for different modes of transportation. In this case, the lack of context can lead to a response that does not adequately address the user's needs.
Consequence: Ambiguity in communication with AI systems can result in confusion, frustration, and wasted time as users try to clarify their intentions or rephrase their queries.

Sometimes, AI systems can misinterpret user intent due to limitations in their understanding of language, context, or cultural nuances. This can lead to responses that are irrelevant, inappropriate, or even offensive.

Example: A user asks an AI system for advice on dealing with a difficult coworker. The AI system may misinterpret the user's request as asking for ways to sabotage the coworker's reputation or career rather than seeking constructive advice for managing the relationship.

Consequence: Misinterpretation of user intent can lead to the AI system providing harmful or misleading information, potentially damaging relationships or causing other negative outcomes.

Another issue that can arise from miscommunication with AI systems is overreliance on their capabilities. Users may assume that AI systems are infallible and blindly trust their responses, even when they may be incorrect or based on incomplete information.

Example: A user relies on an AI-generated financial investment recommendation without considering the system's limitations in understanding market fluctuations, economic indicators, or the user's unique financial situation.
Consequence: Overreliance on AI systems can lead to poor decision-making and negative consequences, such as financial loss or missed opportunities.

AI systems are only as unbiased and ethical as the data they are trained on and the algorithms that govern their behavior. Miscommunication can occur when AI systems inadvertently reinforce biases or perpetuate harmful stereotypes.

Example: A user asks an AI system for suggestions on career paths for women. The AI system, based on historical data or biased training, may suggest traditionally female-dominated professions, thereby reinforcing gender stereotypes.
Consequence: AI systems that reinforce biases or perpetuate stereotypes can perpetuate societal inequalities and contribute to harmful attitudes and beliefs.

Miscommunication with AI systems can have significant consequences, ranging from minor inconveniences to more severe outcomes. To minimize these risks, it is crucial for users to communicate clearly and specifically with AI systems, be aware of their limitations, and critically evaluate the information and recommendations they provide. Additionally, AI developers must continually work to refine AI systems, address biases, and improve their ability to understand and respond to user intent accurately.

2.3: Iteration in AI-Human Communication

Iteration is the process of refining and adjusting our communication with an AI system, based on the responses we receive. This approach allows for a better understanding of the intended message, facilitating a more accurate and meaningful exchange of information.

One of the key reasons why iteration is so crucial in AI-human communication is that it helps to overcome misunderstandings. AI systems might not always fully grasp the subtleties of human language, leading to misinterpretations or incorrect responses. By iterating our questions, instructions, or statements, we can clarify our intent and guide the AI system towards a more accurate understanding of our needs.

Another important aspect of iteration is adapting to the inherent limitations of AI systems. Language models like ChatGPT have certain constraints in their understanding of context, colloquialisms, and complex concepts. By engaging in iterative communication, we can adjust our language, phrasing, or explanations to better accommodate these limitations and obtain the desired information or results. Iteration also plays a significant role in exploring different perspectives. By rephrasing questions or providing additional context, we can prompt AI systems to consider alternative viewpoints or interpretations. This process can lead to new insights, ideas, or solutions that might not have been uncovered otherwise.

Furthermore, iterative communication fosters a more collaborative environment between humans and AI systems. By actively engaging with the AI and refining our communication, we can work together more effectively to improve problem-solving, decision-making, and creative processes.

Lastly, iterative communication offers an opportunity for learning and improvement on both sides of the conversation. As humans and AI systems continue to interact and learn from each other, our understanding of each other's capabilities and limitations can grow, leading to continuous improvement in AI-human communication.

CHAPTER THREE
PRACTICAL APPLICATIONS

Chapter three: Practical Applications

3.1: Utilizing AI Language Models for Content Generation

The applications of AI-generated content span a wide range of fields, including marketing, journalism, and creative writing. In marketing, AI language models have proven useful for generating advertising copy, social media content, email campaigns, and blog posts that effectively engage target audiences. In journalism, these models can assist in drafting news articles, summarizing complex topics, and generating data-driven reports. Moreover, AI-generated content can serve as a source of inspiration for authors in the realm of creative writing, providing prompts, ideas, or even drafts of stories, poems, and other literary works.

To ensure that AI language models generate content that aligns with your goals and brand voice, it is crucial to employ specific techniques. Providing clear prompts and context helps the AI model understand the desired topic, tone, and style of the content. Experimenting with different phrasings, keywords, and input parameters can also help achieve the desired output. Additionally, fine-tuning AI language models with domain-specific datasets or custom vocabulary can further align the generated content with your brand voice or industry.

Evaluating and refining AI-generated content is essential to ensure its quality, relevance, and accuracy. Actively reviewing AI-generated content for factual accuracy, coherence, and relevance to your goals and audience is a vital step. Editing and revising AI-generated content as needed ensures that it aligns with your brand voice, style guidelines, and objectives. Lastly, using feedback and iteration as we saw earlier can improve the AI model's understanding of your requirements and preferences, resulting in more accurate and relevant content generation over time. By following these guidelines, you can effectively harness the potential of AI-generated content in various domains while maintaining quality and consistency.

3.2: Enhancing Business Processes with AI Language Models

AI language models offer numerous benefits across various industries and applications, ranging from sentiment analysis and customer feedback analysis to translation and content moderation.

In the realm of sentiment analysis, customer feedback analysis, and market research, AI language models are invaluable. They can analyze customer reviews, social media comments, or other text data to determine the overall sentiment toward a brand, product, or service. AI-powered solutions can efficiently process and categorize large volumes of customer feedback, identifying trends, pain points, and areas for improvement. Furthermore, AI language models can assist in gathering and analyzing data on competitors, industry trends, and customer preferences to inform strategic decision-making.

AI language models are also instrumental in automating tasks such as document summarization, report generation, and data extraction. These models can generate concise and informative summaries of long or complex documents, such as articles, reports, or legal texts. AI-powered solutions can automate the creation of data-driven reports, visualizations, and insights, saving time and resources. In addition, AI language models can be trained to extract specific information from unstructured text data, such as invoices, contracts, or emails.

Lastly, AI-powered solutions can be implemented for translation, proofreading, and content moderation. AI models can provide fast and accurate translations between multiple languages, facilitating communication and collaboration in a global context. AI-powered tools can detect and correct grammar, spelling, punctuation, and stylistic errors in written content. Moreover, AI language models can help flag and filter inappropriate or harmful content in user-generated text, ensuring a safe and respectful online environment.

By leveraging the capabilities of AI language models, businesses and individuals can streamline their processes, enhance communication, and gain valuable insights from vast amounts of textual data.

3.3: Responsible and Ethical Use of AI Languages Models

The deployment of AI language models comes with potential risks and ethical concerns that must be acknowledged and addressed. Recognizing the possible risks related to bias, privacy, misinformation, and other ethical concerns is essential when deploying AI language models in various applications.
To mitigate biases, ensure privacy, and promote fairness in AI language model applications, several strategies can be employed. Measures to reduce biases in AI-generated content should be implemented, such as using diverse training data and actively monitoring for biased output. Additionally, AI language model applications must respect user privacy and adhere to relevant data protection regulations and guidelines. It is crucial to promote fairness and transparency in AI language model deployment by clearly communicating the capabilities and limitations of the technology.

Responsible and ethical use of AI language models in personal and professional contexts requires adherence to specific guidelines. Following best practices for AI language model use is necessary, such as being transparent about AI-generated content, avoiding harmful applications, and addressing potential biases. Engaging in ongoing dialogue and learning about the ethical implications of AI language models is also vital, as it helps individuals stay informed about emerging concerns and solutions. By adopting a responsible and ethical approach to AI language model deployment, businesses and individuals can harness the power of these technologies while minimizing potential risks and unintended consequences.

3.4: Ideation and Project Planning

The rapid advancement of artificial intelligence (AI) presents companies with tremendous opportunities to revolutionize their business models and unlock new revenue streams. However, successfully integrating AI tools requires generating innovative ideas and implementing these technologies in a strategic and thoughtful manner. In this article, we will discuss the process of generating ideas, implementing AI tools in a company, and adapting business models to leverage the power of AI.
Generating Ideas for AI Integration

The first step in harnessing AI tools is brainstorming ideas for how these technologies can enhance your company's operations, products, or services. Here are some techniques to generate ideas:

- Identify pain points: Analyze your company's processes and identify areas where AI tools could potentially streamline operations, reduce costs, or improve efficiency.
- Explore existing AI applications: Research the ways in which other companies in your industry or related sectors are using AI tools, and consider how similar applications could benefit your organization.
- Encourage collaboration: Organize brainstorming sessions with cross-functional teams to generate ideas and foster a culture of innovation. Encourage employees to think creatively and challenge the status quo.
- Consult with experts: Engage AI experts, consultants, or technology partners to gain insights into the latest developments in AI and potential applications for your company.

Implementing AI Tools in Your Company

Once you have generated a list of potential AI applications, the next step is implementing these tools in your company. Keep the following considerations in mind:

- Develop a strategic roadmap: Create a strategic plan that outlines the objectives, milestones, and resources required for integrating AI tools into your organization. Ensure that the plan aligns with your company's long-term goals and vision.
- Prioritize projects: Evaluate the feasibility, potential impact, and return on investment (ROI) of each AI project idea. Prioritize projects based on these factors and allocate resources accordingly.
- Build an AI-ready workforce: Invest in employee training and development programs to build AI literacy and skills across your organization. This will ensure that your workforce is equipped to handle the changes brought about by AI integration.
- Establish a robust data pipeline. AI tools rely on vast amounts of data to function effectively. Ensure that your company has a solid data infrastructure in place to support the needs of AI applications. How you feed the AI data is a very important point, don't neglect it and don't underestimate it.
- Monitor progress and iterate: Regularly review the performance of AI projects, identifying areas for improvement and making adjustments as needed. This iterative approach will help ensure the success of AI integration efforts.

Adapting Business Models to Leverage AI

Incorporating AI tools into your company's operations may require adapting your business model to fully capitalize on the benefits of these technologies. Consider the following strategies:

- Reimagine products and services: Explore how AI tools can enhance your existing products or services or enable the development of entirely new offerings. This could involve incorporating AI-driven personalization, automation, or predictive analytics into your product or service offerings.
- Optimize processes: Leverage AI tools to optimize internal processes, such as supply chain management, customer support, or human resources, and identify opportunities for cost reduction and efficiency gains.
- Foster strategic partnerships: Form partnerships with AI technology providers or other companies in your industry to jointly develop AI-driven solutions or share resources, knowledge, and expertise.
- Pursue new revenue streams: Identify new market opportunities and revenue streams that emerge as a result of AI integration, such as data-driven insights, AI-powered analytics, or AI-as-a-service offerings.

3.5: Applications and Use Cases of AI Language Models

AI language models have become increasingly powerful and versatile, making them valuable tools for a wide range of applications. In this chapter, we will explore some of the most popular use cases for these models, showcasing their potential to transform various industries and improve our daily lives.

1. Virtual Assistants and Chatbots
One of the most common applications of AI language models is in the creation of virtual assistants and chatbots. These AI-driven helpers can provide customer support, answer questions, and even offer personalized recommendations. By simulating human-like conversation, they can improve user experience and provide valuable assistance across industries such as retail, hospitality, and healthcare.

2. Content Creation and Writing Assistance
AI language models can generate human-like text, making them useful tools for content creation and writing assistance. They can help users draft emails, write articles, or create social media posts by suggesting relevant content, correcting grammar, and offering style suggestions. This can save time and effort while ensuring high-quality, engaging output.

3. Translation Services
Language models have the ability to understand and generate text in multiple languages, making them valuable tools for translation services. They can quickly and

accurately translate text between languages, helping businesses and individuals communicate more effectively across borders and cultures.

4. Sentiment Analysis and Social Media Monitoring
AI language models can be used to analyze large volumes of text, such as social media posts, reviews, and comments, to determine the overall sentiment or mood of the content. This can help businesses monitor their online presence, track customer satisfaction, and identify emerging trends or issues in real-time.

5. Personalized Recommendations
Language models can analyze user preferences, browsing history, and other data to provide personalized recommendations for products, services, or content. This can help businesses improve customer satisfaction and increase sales by offering tailored suggestions that are more likely to resonate with individual users.

6. Natural Language Processing and Understanding
AI language models can be used to process and understand human language in various forms, such as spoken words, written text, or even gestures. This can enable a wide range of applications, from voice-controlled devices and speech recognition software to systems that can analyze and interpret complex documents.

7. Educational Tools
Language models can be used to create interactive, personalized learning experiences for students of all ages. They can provide explanations, answer questions, and even generate practice exercises, helping learners better understand complex concepts and improve their skills. Combined with a text-to-image AI tool for the illustrations, it can offer a great help to make educational content.

8. Code generation and debugging
AI language models can be utilized to generate and complete code snippets, providing developers with suggested solutions for specific coding problems. These models can analyze a given codebase and offer context-aware suggestions based on the programming language, coding style, and project requirements. This can significantly reduce the time and effort required to write new code or modify existing code, allowing developers to focus on more complex tasks and problem-solving.
AI language models can also be employed to identify bugs and potential issues in a codebase. By analyzing patterns and inconsistencies within the code, these models can detect syntax errors, performance issues, or potential security vulnerabilities.
It also had the ability to analyse the code and write documentation.
Documentation is a critical aspect of software development, but it can be time-consuming and challenging to maintain. AI language models can help automate the process of creating and updating documentation, ensuring that it remains accurate, comprehensive, and up-to-date.

In summary, AI language models have a diverse range of applications and use cases, from virtual assistants and chatbots to content creation and translation services. As these models continue to advance, their potential to transform industries and improve our daily lives will only grow.

3.6: Applications and Use Cases of AI Images Generation and Text-to-Image Models

AI image generation and text-to-image models have made significant advancements in recent years. These cutting-edge technologies are now being used in various applications, revolutionizing industries and reshaping the way we interact with digital content. In this chapter, we will explore some of the most popular use cases for AI image generation and text-to-image models.

1. Graphic Design and Art
AI image generation models can create original and visually stunning artwork, enabling artists and designers to push the boundaries of their creativity. These models can generate unique designs, illustrations, or even complete scenes, providing a powerful tool for generating fresh ideas and creating new visual experiences.

2. Advertising and Marketing
AI-generated images can be used to create eye-catching advertisements, promotional materials, and social media posts. By tailoring visuals to specific target audiences, businesses can increase engagement and improve the effectiveness of their marketing campaigns.

3. Concept Visualization
Text-to-image models can generate images from textual descriptions, making them valuable tools for concept visualization. Architects, product designers, and other creative professionals can use these models to quickly generate visual representations of their ideas, facilitating communication and collaboration.

4. Entertainment and Media
AI image generation and text-to-image models can be used to create dynamic and engaging content for movies, video games, and virtual reality experiences. These models can generate realistic characters, environments, and objects, enhancing the overall visual quality and immersing users in captivating virtual worlds.

5. Fashion and Apparel

AI-generated images can be used to design and visualize new clothing, footwear, and accessory items. By generating unique and trendy designs, businesses can stay ahead of the competition and offer consumers fresh and innovative products.

It is also worth mentioning as the technology get more refined, it is now possible to generate fashion photography trough AI. While not perfect yet and limited in resolution compared to a real photo taken on a high-end camera, it can help prepare a shooting and have a better communication inside the company about the results wanted.

6. Data Augmentation and Machine Learning

AI-generated images can be used to augment existing datasets, providing additional training data for machine learning models. This can improve the accuracy and performance of these models, leading to better results in various applications, such as image recognition and object detection.

7. Customizable Avatars and Virtual Assistants

Text-to-image models can be used to create customizable avatars and virtual assistants, allowing users to personalize their digital interactions. By generating avatars based on users' preferences, businesses can create more engaging and relatable experiences for their customers.

CHAPTER FOUR
HOW TO USE CHAT-GPT, MIDJOURNEY AND OTHER AI TOOLS

Chapter Four: How to use ChatGPT, Midjourney and other AI Tools

4.1: ChatGPT – How to make the most of it

ChatGPT is a highly advanced AI language model created by OpenAI, based on the GPT-4 architecture. As a AI companion, its designed to assist you with a wide range of tasks, from answering your questions and providing insightful information to engaging in thought-provoking conversations.
With a knowledge cutoff date of September 2021, it has limited access to the most recent news but we will see this limitation can be solved in some case.

To access ChatGPT, you will to connect to OpenAI website: https://chat.openai.com/

1. Understanding Prompts
In the case of ChatGPT, prompts are short text inputs or questions that you provide to guide the AI in generating a desired response or output. The more specific and clear your prompt, the better ChatGPT can understand your intent and provide a relevant, useful answer.

2. Best practices
Here are some tips to help you create effective prompts and explore the full range of possibilities with ChatGPT:

- Be specific: Provide as much relevant context and information as possible to help the AI understand what you're looking for. For example, instead of asking "What is the best car?", ask "What are the best cars for a family under $30000?"
- Ask follow-up questions: If the initial response doesn't fully address your query, don't hesitate to ask follow-up questions to clarify or narrow down the topic.
- Experiment with different phrasings: If you're not getting the desired response, try rephrasing your prompt or question to make it clearer or more specific.
- Use conversational context: You can establish context by starting a conversation with a brief introduction or background information before asking your main question.
- Combine concepts: Feel free to mix different ideas or concepts in a single prompt to explore creative or unique solutions.

- Request step-by-step instructions or explanations: When seeking guidance or clarification, ask ChatGPT to provide step-by-step instructions or detailed explanations to ensure a thorough understanding.
- Control the response format: You can guide the format of ChatGPT's response by specifying your preference in the prompt, such as "List the top 5 reasons..." or "Explain in a paragraph..."

ChatGPT can also help you code a website or any apps in most of the programming languages used. It can also explain complex things in simple terms and is great at it.

Another powerful way to improve ChatGPT and bypass some of its limitations is to teach him new information. As of today, ChatGPT is not aware of what happened in the world after 2021. However, you can copy paste any articles or text into a prompt and ask him to work on it such as creating a summary, or expanding on the topic.

Being good at prompt and communication with AI will likely be a very sought after skill in the coming years. By understanding and experimenting with these techniques, you can take advantage of the vast capabilities of ChatGPT and discover new ways to engage with the AI, from acquiring knowledge and solving problems to exploring creative ideas and having engaging conversations.

3. Some prompt examples to get your started

To learn something:

- "Identify the 20% of (topic or skill) that will yield 80% of the desired results and provider a focused learning and plan to master it."

- "You are a teacher on (topic or skill). Write me a course about it that could be used in (middle school/high school/university)"

- "Help me create mental models or analogies to better understand and remember key concepts in (topic or skill)"

To write content for your website/media:

- Write an engaging [type of content: tutorial, how-to guide, etc.] on [topic] that helps our [target audience] achieve [specific goal].

- Write a [type of content: script, storyboard, etc.] for a episode about [topic] featuring [guest or expert or characters].

- Write a guest post pitch for [publication or blog] on [topic], demonstrating our [expertise and value proposition].

To help your business:

- Compare [customer satisfaction or feedback data] across [different channels, products, or time periods] to uncover [trends, issues, or opportunities]

- Compare [customer satisfaction or feedback data] across [different channels, products, or time periods] to uncover [trends, issues, or opportunities].

- Write a concise summary of a [brainstorming session] on [topic], including [ideas generated, decisions made, and next steps].

To help you write a fiction:

- Write a scene where (character x) and (character y) discuss (topic)

- Write the outline of a crime drama, make sure to avoid the classic tropes of the genre.

- I have written this, make sure it is grammatically correct: (insert content)

Nb: those examples can also be used in AutoGPT introduced later in this guide, especially for business cases where you need to feed the AI with data from files.

4.2: Midjourney – Text to Image generation guide

Artificial Intelligence (AI) has revolutionized various domains, and one area where its impact is clearly visible is text-to-image generation. Midjourney, a state-of-the-art AI tool is gaining popularity for its incredible ability to convert textual descriptions into high-quality images. In this part, we will explore how to use Midjourney effectively and unleash its full potential for various applications. Also worth mentioning, the cover of the book you are reading was done with the help of Midjourney.

In order to use Midjourney, you will first need a Discord account:
www.discord.com

Discord is a software that allow to chat online, it serves as the user interface to access the AI, it's free. Once the Discord account setup and running, go to www.midjourney.com and click on join the beta:

You will then arrive on the Midjourney Discord channel, feel free to explore it. After looking around, right click on the Midjourney bot on the right of the screen and choose "Send message".

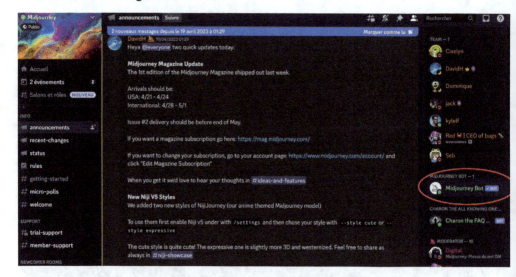

This will start a conversation with the Midjourney bot where you can start writing prompt, always starting with /imagine. Other useful commands to check are /subscribe and /help. Full list available at:
https://docs.midjourney.com/docs/command-list

1. Understanding Prompts
Prompts are short text descriptions or keywords that guide the AI in generating the desired image. Specific and descriptive prompts yield better results, helping the AI understand your intent and produce accurate images.

2. Prompt Structure
Prompts can range from simple single-word phrases to more advanced structures incorporating image URLs, multiple text phrases, and parameters. All prompt will start in Discord with: "/imagine" then the prompt.

3. Prompt Techniques
a. Combine Concepts: Mix artistic mediums, historical periods, locations, and emotions for unique images.

b. Pick a Medium: Specify an artistic medium for a distinct style.
c. Be Specific: Use precise words for the desired look and feel.
d. Time Travel: Experiment with different eras and visual styles.
e. Emote: Add emotions to give characters personality.
f. Get Colorful: Play with color schemes for striking images.
g. Explore Environments: Incorporate different environments to set the mood.
h. Use Parameters: Modify aspect ratios, rendering quality, and other aspects of the image generation process.

Here is an example with the prompt: **Fashion design regency era, man, face, face detail, regency fashion, inside a regency home, England, cinematic, epic scene --v 5**

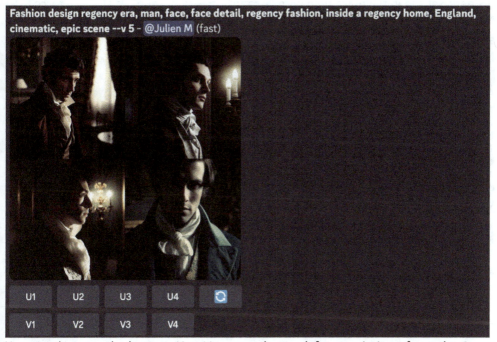

You can then use the buttons U or V to upscale or ask for a variation of one the 4 results.

It is important to note that by specifying --v 5 at the end, we asked Midjourney to use the latest version available, which put emphasis on real life photography. Depending on when you read this book, be sure to check if there is any new version available through the --v parameter. But as of now, if you want characters that look as real as possible, don't forgot to add --v 5 at the end.

4. Parameters Overview

a. Aspect Ratios: Modify the aspect ratio of an image with "--aspect" or "--ar".

b. Chaos: Control the variability of results with "--chaos" or "--c". It can influence on the final result in subtle ways.

c. Quality: Adjust rendering quality using "--quality" or "--q". Beware it might increase rendering time

d. Seed: Set the initial noise field with "--seed" or "--sameseed". It allow to force Midjourney to make new pictures on the same basis as previous one by using the seed number, which is like a reference number linked to each picture generated. More details on this here: https://docs.midjourney.com/docs/seeds

e. Stop: Finish a job partway through the process using "--stop".

f. Stylize: Influence Midjourney's default aesthetic style strength with "--stylize" or "--s".

g. Version: Choose a different version of the Midjourney algorithm using "--version" or "--v".

h. Niji: Generate anime-style images using the "--niji" parameter.

i. Test, Testp, and Creative: Access test models and varied compositions with "--test", "--testp", and "--creative".

You can also use /imagine followed by an image url and text , or a second image url to remix existing content.

5. Parameters examples and use case

a. Aspect Ratios

Example 1: /imagine prompt perfect beach --ar 2:1

Example 2: /imagine prompt perfect beach --ar 1:2

b. Stylize
Example 1: /imagine prompt old city

Example 2: /imagine prompt old city --stylize 800

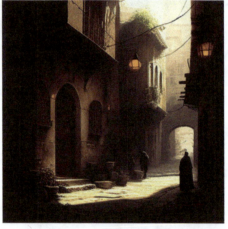

c. Niji
Example: /imagine prompt anime character in a old city --niji

Here are a few examples with their respective prompt to illustrate the capabilities of Midjourney and text to image AI:

A lush forest landscape, a bear, sunrise, Moebius style --ar 21:9 --v 5

A pristine picture of Kyoto under Meiji era with pedestrians, samurai and monks walking in the street --ar 21:9 --v 5

A blue print view of an electric guitar --ar 21:9 --v 5

A fashion model sitting on a travel case near an airplane, beautiful, fashion photography --v 5

sketch version of a wizard character, multiple poses, dark fantasy, serious --ar 21:9 ---v 5

beautiful cosy living room, mountains, fireplace, gothic and classy, lush vegetations, high round windows ar 9:16 --v 5

4.3: Microsoft Bing – Text to Text search engine guide

Microsoft search engine named Bing got updated with a custom version of GPT shared by OpenAI. For the moment it is only accessible by using Microsoft Edge, Microsoft own web browser. You will find it has a Bing AI chatbot sidebar that can be accessed by clicking on the Bing icon on the toolbar. It provides users with quick access to Bing's AI-powered chatbot, which can help users find answers to their questions and provide them with helpful information. It works in similar fashion as ChatGPT but can also react in real time on the content you are browsing on the web. It can be very useful for any academic work or if you need explanations or further details on an article you are reading.

The chatbot from Bing is also directly accessible on www.bing.com if you are using Microsoft Edge or the Bing app on mobile and then click on chat.

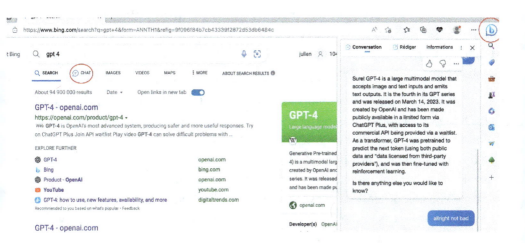

4.4: LLaMa – How to install your own AI on your computer

Before getting into the nitty gritty of the following part, I have to give you a fair warning. This is going to be technical and this specific part about LLaMa is targeted toward software engineers and computer science enthusiasts. But it is worth mentioning since it allow anybody with the skills and a decent computer to work on an artificial intelligence model similar to Chat-GPT. It's a bit like opening the Pandora box. For those who are curious on what is exactly behind things like GPT4 and modern AI in general, it's an amazing opportunity.

But first thing first, what is LLaMa ? LLaMa stand for Large Language Model Meta AI. That's a mouthful so we are going to stick with LLaMa for the rest of this chapter.

LLaMa was developed and trained by Meta AI, the AI branch of Facebook. It works on similar principles as GPT-4. It uses the transformer architecture and was trained on large volume of data, volume only big corporation can afford the time and money for.

It was released on February 23, 2023 under the open-source GPL 3 license, which mean anybody can use it, it's free. But it's important to note that only the model was release at that time. On March 2, 2023, a leak of the weight (the sum of all the training made by Meta AI) was published online. This was significant for all the developer community and curious people out there since training an AI require a lot of time and computer resources than an average people can't have access to. By having finally access to the model and the weight (training data), it was now possible to install an AI on your own computer with decent results.

For obvious legal reason, this guide won't provide you direct link to the weights that were release. If you are curious, they are not hard to find though, magnet links being all over the place. They can also directly be requested to Meta for research use.

Now let's assume you have download LLaMa from Facebook and get the weights package. You will notice there are four data subsets inside. They correspond to different quality (and amount) of data you plug to the model when running it. The size are 7B, 13B, 30B and 65B, B referring to the billions parameters.

I mentioned the need for a decent computer earlier in the chapter. Its due to the fact that those data need to be accessible real time by the AI when it run on your computer, meaning they will load in your RAM. The minimum I would recommend to run the 7B set, is 16 Go of RAM. The more RAM you got the better.

It is also worth noting that technology is evolving really fast and some people managed to lowered considerably the entry barrier to start up LLaMa, running it on smartphone or Raspberry Pi4 for the most extreme cases.

The easiest way to run LLaMa on your computer will be by following the instructions on the Dalai repo on Github: https://github.com/cocktailpeanut/dalai

It will take care of not just starting Llama but also downloading the necessary libraries (including Alpaca) for it to run well. Its cross platform and run on Linux, Mac and Windows.

There is also alternative such as PyLLama that can run the AI on your GPU if it got at least 4gb of VRAM: https://github.com/juncongmoo/pyllama

Then you can decide to fine tuning to your needs. And everything become possible.

A fun example is making your AI talk like Homer Simpson as demonstrated after a short training in this excellent article from Ben Firshman on his blog: https://replicate.com/blog/fine-tune-llama-to-speak-like-homer-simpson

4.5: Auto-GPT – How to try and experiment with GPT 4 full potential

Auto-GPT is an open-source project that takes artificial intelligence to new heights by leveraging the capabilities of the GPT-4 language model. It works by being able to create multiple 'agents' to divide task and plan ahead. This application offers users an unprecedented level of autonomy, enabling them to assign roles and specific objectives to the AI system, which then diligently works to complete the tasks. In short it can prompt itself until the goal you set is complete. Auto-GPT will allow you to build your own personal autonomous assistant that can do pretty much anything.

It's worth noting the project is still work in progress, so crashes may occur.

Throughout the process, users can monitor the AI's thoughts, plans, and progress, while offering feedback or authorizing actions as required. This level of engagement with the AI system provides a unique opportunity for users to experience the future of AI-driven technology, revolutionizing the way we work and interact with these systems.

It is important to mention that it is not like LLaMa seen earlier where the AI is running on your computer. Auto-GPT is an application that allow you to communicate directly with GPT 4, the technology that power ChatGPT. But this time you have much more control on the inputs and outputs. It can do that because it uses the powerful AI directly via API and bypass a lot of the limitations you would find otherwise. It can also follow a plan, and access multiple sources beyond its basic training.

Here is a link to the project: https://github.com/Significant-Gravitas/Auto-GPT

Here is a quick tutorial on how to install it:

Step 1: Install python on your computer

You can download it on python website: https://www.python.org/downloads/

Step 2: Open your terminal on mac or linux. If you are on Windows, install Visual Studio and once its done, open it and access the terminal.
You can download it here: https://visualstudio.microsoft.com/fr/downloads/
Then Use the **View** > **Terminal** menu command.

Step 3: Get the project by typing: `git clone https://github.com/Significant-Gravitas/Auto-GPT.git`

Step 4: Navigate to the project: `cd 'Auto-GPT'`

Step 5: Make sure you are on the stable version: `git checkout stable`

Step 6: Rename `.env.template` to `.env` and fill in your `OPENAI_API_KEY`.
Obtain your OpenAI API key from: https://platform.openai.com/account/api-keys.
Beware using your api key will require you to setup a payment card in the billing menu.

Step 7: This one is optional. You can setup what you want the AI to do by editing the file `ai_settings.yaml`. You can also skip this step, and can set up the role and goals when you launch the application in the step 8

Example:
ai_name: William Wallace
ai_role: AI-driven history teacher
ai_goals:
- Create a 5 pages lesson that cover the History of Scotland between the 8th century and the 13th century and save it in a file name Scotland.txt.
- Create an exam test as a companion the lesson previously written and save it in a file exam.txt.
- Calculate the cost of a field trip of 3 days in Edinburg for a class of 20 students leaving from London. They travel by bus.

Step 8: Launch AutoGPT: `./run.sh` or if you on Windows `.\run.bat`
After each of Auto-GPT's actions, you will be asked if you want to continue with the next command by answering y (yes) or n(no). You can let it work until it finish his task by writing: y -30
This will let it run the next 30 commands by itself.

You can see how it is display when running as a movie critic in the capture below:

```
Welcome to Auto-GPT! Enter the name of your AI and its role below. Entering nothing will load defaults.
Name your AI: For example, 'Entrepreneur-GPT'
AI Name: Movie critique
Movie critique here! I am at your service.
Describe your AI's role: For example, 'an AI designed to autonomously develop and run businesses with the sole goal of increasing your net worth.'
Movie critique is: An AI designed to write movies review
Enter up to 5 goals for your AI: For example: Increase net worth, Grow Twitter Account, Develop and manage multiple businesses autonomously'
Enter nothing to load defaults, enter nothing when finished.
Goal 1: write a movie review of the movie 'Evil Dead Rise' and save it in the file EDRreview.txt.
Goal 2: write a article about the Evil Dead franchise
Goal 3:
Using memory of type: LocalCache
MOVIE CRITIQUE THOUGHTS: As a movie critique, I should begin with writing a review of the recently released film 'Evil Dead Rise'. However, I may n
eed to do some research on the movie first to form an informed opinion. I will start with a Google search to gather more information about the movi
e.
REASONING: Google search will be the best first command to search for information on the movie.
PLAN:
-  Perform a Google search for 'Evil Dead Rise'.
-  Scan through the information gathered to form an informed opinion on the movie.
-  Then I will proceed to write the review of the movie and save it in the file EDRreview.txt.
CRITICISM: I need to remember to scan through the information gathered carefully to get the right information for the movie review.
```

This is just an example and by no mean should be taken as face value. AutoGPT is not a replacement for a real history teacher or a movie critic. It's up to you to be creative and invent new way to use this tool. But to sum it up, it can do a lot more than ChatGPT.

There is also a more user-friendly alternative. You can access it on the website:
https://godmode.space
It has a user interface similar to ChatGPT but work like AutoGPT. It will also require you API key from OpenAI. You can with a push of a button allowing it to be autonomous for the next 10 minutes and it is a great way to get use to this type of AI.

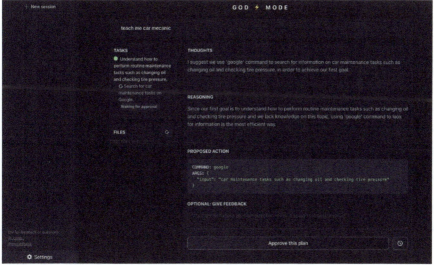

4.6: Other AI Tools

The current pace of innovation and new products coming to the market of artificial intelligence is astounding. What follow is a quick introduction to the other tools available as of early 2023. Most of them are in beta.

Adobe Firefly

Adobe Firefly, a generative AI launched in March 2023, offers groundbreaking creative tools in its beta mode. Users can experiment with text-to-image transformations, generate unique text styles and textures, and soon, recolor vector graphics using text prompts.
https://www.adobe.com/sensei/generative-ai/firefly.html

DALL.E2

DALL·E2 is a generative AI model that creates images from textual descriptions. It is a variant of the GPT model, specifically designed for image generation. By inputting a text prompt, DALL·E2 can generate a wide range of visual content, including objects, animals, scenes, and abstract concepts. This AI has demonstrated remarkable capabilities in producing coherent and contextually relevant images based on the provided descriptions, but also providing outpainting, inpainting and variations.
https://openai.com/product/dall-e-2

Stable Diffusion

Stable Diffusion, a deep learning text-to-image model launched in 2022, is developed by Stability AI in collaboration with academic researchers and non-profit organizations. It generates detailed images based on text descriptions and handles tasks like inpainting, outpainting, and image-to-image translations guided by text prompts. As a latent diffusion model, its code and model weights are publicly available, and it runs on consumer hardware with a modest GPU. This contrasts with proprietary models like DALL-E and Midjourney, which are accessible only through cloud services.
https://stablediffusionweb.com

Bard

Google Bard is a sophisticated AI chatbot created by Google, stemming from the LaMDA family of expansive language models. Designed as a direct competitor to OpenAI's ChatGPT, Google Bard made its debut in a limited release in March 2023. It had a mitigated reception so far. It is also not widely available.
https://bard.google.com

Jarvis

Jarvis is a Microsoft Git project that employs a large language model (LLM) as a controller and multiple expert models from HuggingFace Hub as executors. The system features a four-stage workflow: task planning with ChatGPT, model selection based on descriptions, task execution with chosen models, and response generation by integrating model predictions.
https://github.com/microsoft/JARVIS

Gen2 Ai

Runway's Gen2 AI, a cutting-edge solution for realistic and consistent video synthesis. The technology offers two powerful approaches: Video-to-Video and Text-to-Video. In Video-to-Video, the composition and style of an image or text prompt are applied to the structure of a source video, transforming it seamlessly. Alternatively, Text-to-Video synthesis generates entirely new videos based on textual descriptions, opening up a world of possibilities for creative visual content with just a few words.
https://research.runwayml.com/gen2

Synthesia

Synthesia is an advanced AI video generation platform, allowing users to effortlessly produce videos featuring AI avatars in more than 120 languages. The platform comes equipped with a range of tools, including templates, a screen recorder, and a media library, streamlining the video creation process and making it more accessible to users across the globe.
https://www.synthesia.io

Tome.app

Tome.app is an AI-assisted storytelling platform designed to facilitate the creation of narratives by integrating video, interactivity, and live data. Ideal for crafting presentations, Tome.app's integration with Figma and incorporation of live web content offer a dynamic and interactive storytelling experience.
https://beta.tome.app

Claude

Claude, developed by Anthropic, is a text-to-text AI adept at handling large volumes of text. It performs tasks like editing, rewriting, summarizing, and extracting data. Claude engages in natural conversations, possesses extensive general knowledge, and supports multiple languages, including programming languages. Its automation capabilities streamline basic instructions and logical scenarios.
https://www.anthropic.com/index/introducing-claude

Copilot

GitHub Copilot, trained on billions of lines of code, converts natural language prompts into coding suggestions for numerous languages. By writing a comment outlining the desired logic, Copilot instantly proposes code to implement the solution. Seamlessly integrating into editors such as Neovim, JetBrains IDEs, Visual Studio, and Visual Studio Code, Copilot is fast enough to provide real-time assistance as you type. It's based on OpenAi technology.
https://github.com/features/copilot

Descript

Descript revolutionizes podcast production with its user-friendly approach, setting it apart from traditional complex audio tools. It employs AI to automatically transcribe uploaded audio, allowing users to edit recordings by simply highlighting, deleting, or moving words or passages in a text editor. Descript streamlines the podcast creation process, making it accessible and efficient.
https://www.descript.com

CHAPTER FIVE
FUTURE DEVELOPMENTS AND TRENDS IN AI

Chapter Five: Future Developments and Trends in AI

5.1: Advance in AI Language Model Technologies

In the future, we can expect significant developments and trends in AI language models. It's essential to stay informed about the latest advancements in AI language model architectures, such as new transformer-based models or innovations in recurrent neural networks (RNNs). These advancements have the potential to impact the performance, capabilities, and applications of AI language models.

There are also emerging techniques for training and fine-tuning AI language models. These cutting-edge techniques, such as unsupervised or self-supervised learning, can improve the efficiency and effectiveness of these models. It's crucial to investigate new methods for fine-tuning AI language models, including techniques that can enhance domain-specific expertise or address challenges like few-shot learning.

Another area to watch is the development of AI language models with multilingual and cross-lingual capabilities. These models can process and generate text in multiple languages or enable communication between speakers of different languages.

Also as documented by Microsoft, AI researchers have made significant progress in developing large language models (LLMs) like GPT-4, which exhibit more general intelligence than previous AI models. These models, including ChatGPT and Google's PaLM, demonstrate remarkable capabilities across various domains and tasks, such as mathematics, coding, vision, medicine, law, and psychology. Their performance is strikingly close to human-level and often surpasses prior models like ChatGPT.

GPT-4 has been trained using an unprecedented scale of compute and data, and its early version could be considered a step towards Artificial General Intelligence (AGI). However, researchers are still working on understanding its limitations and exploring new paradigms to achieve deeper and more comprehensive versions of AGI.
As AI language models continue to advance, it's crucial to consider the societal implications of these technological leaps and identify future research directions that ensure responsible and beneficial development.

Staying up-to-date on advancements in this area will help us understand the implications of these developments for global communication, collaboration, and accessibility. By keeping an eye on these trends and developments, we can better understand and leverage the power of AI language models to benefit various applications and industries.

5.2: The Alignment Problem

The Alignment Problem is a significant concern in the development of Artificial General Intelligence (AGI) and AI systems. It refers to the challenge of aligning AI's goals and decision-making processes with human values and intentions. The crux of the issue lies in ensuring that advanced AI systems act in a manner that is beneficial to humans and does not lead to unintended consequences. As AI becomes more capable and autonomous, the risk of misaligned objectives increases, potentially resulting in AI systems that act against human interests or cause harm. Addressing the Alignment Problem is crucial for the safe development and deployment of AGI and other advanced AI systems, requiring interdisciplinary collaboration from researchers, ethicists, and policymakers to create robust and value-aligned AI solutions.

5.3: The Evolving AI Ecosystem and Industry Landscape

The AI language model landscape is constantly changing, with new providers, platforms, and tools emerging in the market. It's essential to monitor these developments to make informed decisions about which solutions best suit your needs. Collaborative efforts, partnerships, and joint ventures between AI language model providers, technology companies, and other stakeholders can have significant impacts on the development, accessibility, and applications of AI language models. Regulatory frameworks and policy developments, such as data protection laws, AI ethics guidelines, and industry-specific regulations, can influence the use and deployment of AI language models. Understanding these policy developments ensures compliance and responsible use of the technology.

Currently, major companies like OpenAI, Microsoft, Google, Meta, and Amazon dominate the AI language model market. As competition increases, the cost of development is expected to decrease, making it more affordable for developers to build on these platforms. Advances in the efficiency of training and serving models will also contribute to performance improvements and cost reductions. Open-source models and proprietary models are diverging in capabilities and cost.

While open-source models can provide a cheaper and more customizable alternative, they may lag behind proprietary models in performance due to the high cost of training and access to proprietary datasets. Developers will need to choose between cutting-edge proprietary models or more affordable open-source alternatives.

As AI models grow in size and complexity, they exhibit more emergent behavior, leading to new applications and use cases that are currently unpredictable. This trend is both exciting and challenging, as businesses built on specific AI capabilities may need to adapt to the rapid emergence of new features in next-generation models. The unpredictability of emergent behavior also means that the path to artificial general intelligence (AGI) is uncertain and may accelerate faster than expected. It is essential to stay informed about advancements in AI and be prepared to adapt to the ever-changing landscape of AI language models.

5.4: Preparing for the Future of AI Language Models in Your Organization

Adopting AI language models in your organization can bring both opportunities and challenges. To identify the potential benefits, risks, and challenges, consider factors such as your industry, company size, and existing technology infrastructure. The adoption process may involve different AI uses, such as text-to-text, API, or other AI applications, depending on your business needs.

Develop a strategic roadmap to integrate AI language models into your organization, outlining key milestones, resources, and success metrics. Incorporate AI language models into your long-term business strategies and vision, considering how these technologies may shape your organization's future growth and competitive advantage.

Cultivating an AI-ready workforce and fostering a culture of innovation is crucial for the successful adoption of AI language models. Invest in employee training and development programs to build AI literacy and skills across your organization. This is a key point in order to maximize AI usage and also making sure you can troubleshoot basic issues and errors that may occur, especially during the transition phase. Encourage a culture of innovation and experimentation, providing opportunities for employees to engage with AI language models and contribute to their successful adoption and use. By embracing AI language models in your organization, you can stay ahead of the competition and drive growth in the rapidly evolving world of AI technology.

5.5: AI Language Models and the Future of Work

Throughout history, humans have held a deep belief in their uniqueness and superiority, but advancements in science and technology have constantly challenged this notion. Discoveries in animal behavior and the development of increasingly intelligent machines have gradually debunked the idea of human exceptionalism. Today, the rapid progress in AI language models raises questions about the future of work and the value of human intelligence and creativity in a world where machines are becoming more sophisticated.

The singularity, the moment when computers meet and exceed human intelligence, is fast approaching. As AI language models continue to develop and exhibit advanced capabilities, various industries and professions will be affected. Some domains will still value human input, while others will see human skill as costly and extraneous. The introduction of AI will undoubtedly lead to job losses, wealth disparities, and shifts in the workforce. However, with political will and collective effort, society might be able to address these challenges and reduce inequality.

Large language models, such as ChatGPT, have displayed remarkable abilities in generating realistic, coherent, and context-sensitive text. As with any new technology that automates a skill, AI language models will impact those who offer that skill in the market. Drawing parallels with the introduction of word processing programs in the 1980s, certain jobs will disappear while new roles will emerge, fostering productivity and innovation.

Despite their impressive capabilities, AI language models have limitations. They require human intervention to craft appropriate prompts, may generate inappropriate or nonsensical outputs, and lack abstract understanding of truth, falsehood, and common sense. These shortcomings present opportunities for creative and knowledge workers who can adapt and integrate AI language models into their work.

To thrive in the future of work, professionals must be willing to prompt, guide, collate, curate, edit, and augment machine-generated outputs. Specialized and technical language will remain largely inaccessible to machines, and new roles will emerge, such as fine-tuning AI language models for specific industries and markets.

The development of AI language models will undoubtedly disrupt the workforce, but it also presents valuable opportunities for those willing to adapt and integrate these powerful tools. As we move into an era of widely accessible AI models, the question remains whether society will seize this moment to promote equity or allow disparities to widen. The future of work depends on our ability to navigate this new landscape, balancing the potential of AI language models with the inherent value of human intelligence and creativity.

Conclusion

As we reach the end of our journey together, it's incredible to see just how far we've come. From understanding the basics of AI to delving into the intricacies of language models like ChatGPT and GPT-4, we've discovered the potential of these technologies to transform our lives, industries, and society as a whole.

In writing this book, it is important to acknowledge the assistance provided by ChatGPT, an AI language model that played a significant role in organizing content, ideas, and insights throughout the text and Midjourney who helped making the cover. This collaboration demonstrates the potential of AI to enhance human creativity and aid in the production of valuable knowledge.

But while we celebrate the marvels of AI, we must also be mindful of the responsibility that comes with wielding such power. As AI continues to progress, we face ethical challenges related to privacy, security, and the potential displacement of human labor. It's crucial that we address these issues and ensure that AI serves as a force for good, benefiting everyone in society.

Thank you for joining me on this exploration of AI and its impact on our world. I hope that this book has inspired you to think critically about the role AI can play in your own life, work, and society, and that you will continue to engage with and contribute to the exciting developments that lie ahead in the world of artificial intelligence.

Bibliography

"Sparks of Artificial General Intelligence" (March 2023). Sébastien Bubeck , Varun Chandrasekaran, Ronen Eldan, Johannes Gehrke , Eric Horvitz , Ece Kamar , Peter Lee , Yin Tat Lee , Yuanzhi Li, Scott Lundberg, Harsha Nori, Hamid Palangi , Marco Tulio Ribeiro , Yi Zhang. Available at: https://www.microsoft.com/en-us/research/publication/sparks-of-artificial-general-intelligence-early-experiments-with-gpt-4/

"History of Artificial Intelligence" (March 2023). Wikipedia. Available at: https://en.wikipedia.org/wiki/History_of_artificial_intelligence

"Auto-GPT: An Autonomous GPT-4 Experiment" (March 2023). Torance Bruce Richards. Available at: https://github.com/Significant-Gravitas/Auto-GPT

"Fine-tune LLaMA to speak like Homer Simpson" (March 2023). Ben Firshman. Available at: https://replicate.com/blog/fine-tune-llama-to-speak-like-homer-simpson

"PyLLaMA - Run LLM in A Single 4GB GPU" (March 2023). Juncong Moo . Available at: https://github.com/juncongmoo/pyllama

"Dalai" (March 2023). Cocktailpeanut. Available at: https://github.com/cocktailpeanut/dalai

"Midjourney Documentation" (February 2023). Available at: https://docs.midjourney.com/docs

"Planning for AGI and beyond" (February 2023). Sam Altman. Available at: https://openai.com/blog/planning-for-agi-and-beyond

Acknowledgments

My brother for his precious advices and being an awesome human being

My dad for allowing me to use a computer when I was 8. I was hooked.

Notes

"The true sign of intelligence is not knowledge but imagination." - Albert Einstein